# Look What the Lord Made

Written by

MIRTHELL BAZEMORE

Edited by

Sis. Sandra J. Gregg

Illustrated by

Keatin J. Tisdale

*AuthorHouse™*
*1663 Liberty Drive*
*Bloomington, IN 47403*
*www.authorhouse.com*
*Phone: 1 (800) 839-8640*

*Published by AuthorHouse 07/27/2018*

*ISBN: 978-1-5462-5234-4 (sc)*
*ISBN: 978-1-5462-5235-1 (e)*

*Print information available on the last page.*

*Any people depicted in stock imagery provided by Getty Images are models,*
*and such images are being used for illustrative purposes only.*
*Certain stock imagery* © *Getty Images.*

*This book is printed on acid-free paper.*

*Because of the dynamic nature of the Internet, any web addresses or links contained in this book may have changed*
*since publication and may no longer be valid. The views expressed in this work are solely those of the author and do not*
*necessarily reflect the views of the publisher, and the publisher hereby disclaims any responsibility for them.*

author**HOUSE**®

# Dedicated to

## The Church In the Lord Jesus Christ of the Apostles' Doctrine

Bishop Joe C. Tisdale, Pastor

"The Little Flock"

# Acknowledgements

Thank you to my church family for your love, encouragement and most of all prayers. It is an honor to share my God given talent to glorify our Lord and Savior Jesus Christ and inspire others along the way.

Special thanks, to Bishop Joe C. Tisdale, Mother Diana Tisdale, Min.Gainwell Smith, Bro.Lionel Bazemore, Bro.Victor South, Sis. Sheila South, Sis. Sandra J. Gregg, Vyone Tisdale Showers, Deacon Quintin Tisdale, Sis. Shandra Tisdale, Sis. Pamela Wright and De'Angelo Wright, Jr.

Lastly, proceeds from this book will be donated to
The Church In the Lord Jesus Christ of the Apostles' Doctrine.
Hartsville, SC
www.thechurchin.org

Making a difference with the gift the Lord blessed me with,
One book at a time...
Sis. Mirthell Bazemore

"Lo, children are an heritage of the LORD"

There is a little boy name Junior who lives with
his grandma.
He always enjoys spending time with her because of
the love and care she shows him.

Junior often goes to church with his Grandma to hear about the Lord.

The church he attends with her happens to be
The Church in the Lord Jesus Christ of the
Apostles' Doctrine.

Junior often hears his grandma say,
"Praise the Lord" and he hears her calling on the name
of the Lord.

This sparks Junior's interest in wanting to know–
Who is this Lord?

One particular Sunday morning, Grandma had
awakened her grandson to prepare him for church.
As she drew back the curtains,
the sun shone brightly on Little Junior's innocent face.

It shone so radiantly that little Junior was amazed
by its brightness.
He asked,"Grandma, who made the Sun?"
She replied, "The Lord Jesus did, Junior"

After eating breakfast that morning, Grandma got little Junior ready for church.

"Time to brush your teeth and wash your face"
said grandma.

Now, the two of them were on their way to church.
While strolling along, Junior noticed a bird sitting on a
fence
chirping loudly as if it was PRAISING the Lord!
It was the most beautiful blue bird he had ever seen.

He asked his grandma,
"Who made that beautiful blue bird?"
Grandma smile and replied, "The Lord Jesus did."
Junior looked up in amazement and ask her,
"He made the birds, too?"
Her answer was Yes! "The Lord made everything"
He just smiled and walked along with her.

As they continued to walk along, a beautiful butterfly
appeared and landed gently on a flower.
Junior asked again, "Who made the butterfly?"
Grandma said, "The Lord did."

"Grandma," Junior asked again, "Who made the green grass?"
She replied, "The Lord made the grass and He made the flowers too."

She continued to help her grandson understand the beauty and might of God almighty by telling him, He made the animals.

## "He made the clouds"

He made the snow, rain, oceans, rivers, and lakes.

He made the fish, whales, dolphins, and sharks.
In fact, the Lord made all living and nonliving things.
What a wonderful God we serve!

She also said, "God made the moon to give us
light in darkness"

Finally, Grandma said, "You know what Junior, God made you and he made me."
Junior replied, "Wow, Grandma, the Lord made everything!"
And so he did.

As soon as the two of them reached the front door
of the church, Junior turned to grandma and said,
"Grandma, I want to meet the Lord one day."
She hugged him and said, "You know what,
I can't wait to meet him, also."

Junior could not wait to get to church to tell the Bishop about all the beautiful things he had seen that the Lord has made.


What a wonderful God we serve!


THE END!!!

# About the Illustrator

*Keatin Jaycee Tisdale* is currently an eighth grader interested in drawing, reading, and basketball. He is a member of the Junior Beta Club and volunteers in his community.

Keatin was admitted into The Tri-District Arts Consortium (Tri-DAC). A program designed to serve artistically gifted and talented students.

Keatin attends The Church in the Lord Jesus Christ of the Apostles' Doctrine. He is the son of Deacon Quintin Tisdale and Sister Shandra Tisdale.

His grandparents are Mr. and Mrs. Thomas Williams; and

Bishop Joe C. Tisdale and Mother Diana Tisdale.

# About the Author

"Making a difference with the gift God gave me"

*Mirthell Bazemore* is a published author and a native of Northern California which currently resides in South Carolina; She is a member of The Church In the Lord Jesus Christ of the Apostles' Doctrine.

Passionate about encouraging others to exercise their gift of writing, she enjoys glorifying the Lord in written word.

To find out more about her projects visit her website at
www.mirthellbazemore.com

Working in God's vineyard, while giving praise to the Lord!

Look what the Lord made is about a little boy's journey and discovery about all the wonderful things God created. While traveling to church with his beloved grandmother, he is shown some of the Great Works of our Lord and Savior, Jesus Christ.
A great starter book for children age 2 and up.

Printed in the United States
By Bookmasters